Summary of

Rich Dad's Cashflow Quadrant:

By: Robert T Kiyosaki

Proudly Brought to you by:

Text Copyright © Readtrepreneur

Legal & Disclaimer

damages or injury caused by the use and application, whether directly or indirectly, of any advice or information presented, whether for breach of contract, tort, negligence, personal injury, criminal intent, or under any other cause of action.

You agree to accept all risks of using the information presented inside this book. You need to consult a professional medical practitioner in order to ensure you are both able and healthy enough to participate in this program.

Table of Contents

The Book at a Glance

What is your ultimate objective in life?

This question is important because your goal in life should also be your path in life. This goal should consume your every thought, encourage your every action and instill every habit that will lead you to achieving the things you want.

Take Robert Kiyosaki for example. Going to school was not his ultimate objective in life. In fact, it was far from it. Sure, he went to military school and spent four years of his life there. He studied so much in order to be a qualified ship's officer. But this was not his path in life. There was no passion in this endeavor. At the end of the day, the school was just a preparation for the rest of his life.

Sadly, this is true for many people nowadays. The path of life that most people follow is very predictable. Go to school, get good grades, and then have a secure, risk-free and tenured job. Their ambition rests in the E quadrant or S quadrant and often stays there forever. Their financial plan is to save up all their salaries and live like a monk. Many depend their retirement on the government's social security or their company's retirement plan (such as 401(k)) and pray to the heavens that the market will not crash when they reach that particular age.

If they are lucky, they may get a measly lump sum from this that would finance their lifestyle for the next five to ten years. But what will happen if they live beyond those ten years? Where will they get money then? How about those old dreams of travelling the world and retiring young? Truly, becoming a player in the E quadrant or S quadrant is not the solution if one's problem is to attain true financial freedom.

This is the primary purpose of this book: to teach you the **CASHFLOW Quadrant** and help you use it to your advantage.

Understanding CASHFLOW Quadrant is important because it will give you a financial path to follow life. You already know that most people today are like robots because they are pre-programmed by society, by their parents and by the traditions. They do not know what to think, how to think and when to think. In other words, their path to life was already set and they are just going through the motions. Their destiny is dim and they have no other ambitions beyond wanting to please other people.

CASHFLOW Quadrant, on the other hand, will give you another route. It will provide a path to mastery and another manner with which to enrich your life. It will give you an edge over the others who are stuck as employees in the E quadrant or as professionals in the S quadrant. It will help you understand how the choices that you make now, the ones which are solely for yourself, can turn the course of your life and lead you to that financial freedom you desire.

Should we get started?

Chapter 1

WHY DON'T YOU GET A JOB?

Robert Kiyosaki, together with his wife Kim, were going through homelessness back in 1985. At the time, they had no cash savings in the bank whatsoever and were unemployed. In the eyes of everyone, they were "losers" with no chance of recovering.

Sure, they can always go back to corporate America and be employees; considering that they both had degrees as well as good work habits. If they followed that path, they would have a high-paying and stable job that would give more to them than just food on the table. However, they were looking for security. At that point in time, Robert and Kim were looking for financial freedom and they knew that they could not get it by being a corporate employee, constantly hoping to rise up the ranks through years and years of hard work.

Sure, the beginning was rough, but because of this gamble, they became successful.

By 1989, Robert and Kim were millionaires. At that point, many people will consider them already as financially successful and will not work further! The couple, however, had other plans. Although they had millions of dollars sitting in the bank, it is not yet sufficient to say that they have achieved true financial freedom. They wanted MORE. By 1999, they were finally FINANCIALLY FREE. By that time, they no longer needed to work a day in their lives.

How did they do this?

They took advantage of the CASHFLOW QUADRANT, which is represented by the diagram below:

The symbol E stands for employee
The symbol S stands for small business or self-employed
The symbol B stands for big business (500 employees)
The symbol I stands for investor

Each quadrant simply represents the unique ways by which income is gained by a person. For instance, an employee who works for the Government or for a Private Corporation earns a salary in exchange for the hours he renders per day, which usually consists of 8 hours, and is otherwise known as the 9-5 job (E Quadrant).

An accountant who works from a list of clients who need auditing services earns professional income in exchange for the service he provides without any employer-employee relationship between them (S Quadrant). An owner of a McDonald's franchise, in a high traffic place in Orange County, California earns money from the profits he acquired as a result of the revenues raised by his active operation of the business, which is done by selling hamburgers and fries to other people (B Quadrant). An investor in Berkshire, Hathaway earns money from the investments made and personally managed by Warren Buffet and Charlie Munger without any active participation on the part of the investor (I Quadrant).

In other words, there are different methods for earning money, just like there are different Quadrants. You can choose to earn money in one quadrant, two quadrants, three quadrants, or all four quadrants simultaneously. Or, you can choose to earn money from each of the quadrants successively, such as when you start as an employee of a corporation, then start your own personal service firm where you do all the work, then move on to creating a corporation where your officers and workers do the heavy duty and the end goal is to become a passive investor, in which you are merely waiting for the check arising from the profits of the investments you made.

Different quadrants are also dependent on one's technical skills, educational attainment, and outlook in life, frames of mind and overall temperament. As they say, different strokes for different folks. Thus, different kinds of people will be magnetized to different kinds of quadrants.

Chapter Two

DIFFERENT QUADRANTS, DIFFERENT PEOPLE

The people categorized in the different quadrants are all different. They have different levels of aversion to risks, different likes and dislikes, different lifestyles and different outlooks towards life, career and relationships.

Now, how can you determine head on if the person you are talking to is from the E quadrant, S quadrant, B quadrant, or I quadrant without having background knowledge over them?

The answer is simple. Observe the words they are speaking. In this way, you can easily determine their needs and wants, and deal with them effectively in the least amount of time.

What do people from the E quadrant usually say?

- I am working for this company for so long and I deserve a pay raise!

- I am working for this company for so long and I deserve a promotion!

- I worked for his dad and now I work for him, loyalty must mean something, right? I want to be promoted.

- At this point in my life I just want a position that is secure and will not be taken away from me by any young employee.

- I want to be in this job because the owner said that if I stay here for the rest of my career the retirement benefits are amazing.

- I want to be in an office where I can enjoy security of tenure.

What do people from the S quadrant usually say?

- I cannot delegate because people usually shortchange the customer or client.

- I cannot delegate because it will mean I have to teach and train youngsters and it takes so much time and effort to do that.

- They cannot simply do it properly. Thus, I might as well do it myself.

- As a real estate broker, my commission for every sold piece of real property in California is 6%.

- As a medical practitioner, my rate for every medical check-up and diagnosis is $xxx.

- As a legal practitioner, my acceptance fee is $xxx. This acceptance shall include all my efforts to study your files and documents and the legal remedies available in accordance with the applicable rules, statute and jurisprudence. My appearance fee for every hearing of the case shall be $xxx.

- It will take me period of two hours to construct the leaked faucet in your condominium unit. By the way, I charge $xxx per hour.

What do people from the B quadrant usually say?

- I am looking for a new manager for the sales department. I need someone who has worked here for a number of years already and has tremendous experience in this industry. In other words, I need an in house applicant.

- I would like to appoint you as the new CEO-President of my company as long as you will prove to me that you have an MBA in an Ivy League Institution.

7

What do people from the I quadrant usually say?

- How much is the annual rate of return of that investment?

- How can we avail of tax exemptions for my investments?

- What is the best way to take advantage of the recession? What severely underpriced assets can we purchase that has a great cash flow?

- How can we take advantage of the recent real estate bubble within the economy? Should we buy apartment units and pay off the outstanding loan of its original buyers?

Chapter Three

WHY PEOPLE CHOOSE SECURITY OVER FREEDOM

What is the primary reason why people seek job security over financial freedom?

It is simple, people were socially conditioned and brainwashed to choose security at all times over freedom. Who taught them these things? The common culprits are the teachers and the school system, their parents and grandparents who did not know any better, the multinational corporations and especially the media (including the Hollywood movies).

The value of security over freedom was instilled in children from a very young age. Imagine, is there a course or even a lesson about financial literacy and building businesses when you were younger? Of course not! Instead, you were taught to conform to the system which emphasizes good grades above anything else. The result of this conformist thinking is a loyal and competent employee who cannot think for himself. The sad thing is that they still follow this advice even when they become fully functioning adults!

Closely observe the CASHFLOW Quadrant below. By doing so, you will realize that the people represented by the left side of the spectrum are primarily encouraged to act in accordance with their goals of having a safe, secure and risk-free life. Comparably, the people represented by the right side are motivated by freedom and having to live their life on their own terms:

It's clear that the people representing the E quadrant and the S quadrant are primarily focused on making sure that they have secure sources of income through active means. It is likewise beneficial to know the reason why they are trapped in this quadrant during the start of their adulthood and even for the entire duration of their adulthood!

They learned in school, especially in the university system, that being secure in one's job is the way to go about life. The frustrating thing is that high school graduates are often encouraged and persuaded (to their own peril but without any warning whatsoever) to avail of college loans in order to attend a "prestigious university."

What these students do not know is that the college loan that they availed is an albatross contract that they will have to pay up immediately after graduation, if they do not want to be in debt forever. This so-called college loans are coupled with massive interest rates that an entry-level employee cannot easily pay off within one year. Thus, these young adults have to pay them for several years sometimes even spanning decades in jobs or professions that they hate doing but are "secure." The end result is a depressed workforce who cannot afford to take a day off on their job lest they miss on paying their college loans.

After successfully paying the loans, the person will now have an opportunity to start saving for his or her financial future. But the reality is that they are not taught how to save! Thus, instead of saving his or her income, he/she will spend it on things. More often than not, since he/she deprived himself/herself several years back, he/she will definitely splurge on often unnecessary things.

Therefore, this is the time when he/she buys a house, gadgets, some luxuries, some new clothes, furniture and automobile.

Soon enough, he/she is again trapped in debt. Soon he/she will get married and will have an expensive wedding. Again, since he/she has no savings, he/she will avail a loan in order to finance the dream wedding! Soon enough, the couple is financially strapped again because their income is not sufficient to pay all the outstanding loans.

This is the time when they begin wishing for financial literacy. This is also the time when they realize that they were sold a wrong dream and were taken advantage of by the system. They recognize the fact that had they used the money they earned at the start of their career in order to start a business or invest, they would have a sizeable time by retirement time (by being in the B and I quadrants). Instead, they pushed themselves and worked like a horse in a work environment that they do not like just to pay up the loans that are due every month. This is an unending cycle of debt, money, frustrations and depressions.

Chapter Four

THE THREE KINDS OF BUSINESS SYSTEMS

Your goal must be to create a unique system that will enable people to work for you, every working day so that you will be able to successfully move to the B quadrant. In order to do this, you need to create a business system for yourself, utilize or exploit someone else's system and purchase and make use of an already available system.

So why do you need a business system in the first place? Simply put, you need the system because it will enable you to make the dramatic shift from S Quadrant or E Quadrant into the B Quadrant. Think of a business system as your highway towards financial freedom and wealth building.

That is, in order to get from A to B, you need to use the highway (business system) in order to get to place B (financial freedom). It is dependent on your own preference how fast you want to go to reach that goal. You can stay to choose in your place A forever (S quadrant and E quadrant). You can walk towards that place B, or you can use a vehicle. You can likewise choose what vehicle to use – you can use a bike, a motorcycle or a car. You can also use an airplane if you want to get there even faster!

If you so choose a car to get to place B (financial freedom), you can further choose to create a car model for yourself (traditional corporation), use the car model of another and utilize its machine (franchising) or purchase a car model that is already mass produced and sold by Toyota, Hyundai or Ford (network marketing). Everything is up to you!

With that in mind, you've just learned the 3 main categories of business systems that are commonly used by people in the S quadrant and E quadrant in order to get to the B quadrant!

One thing to keep in mind with respect to Traditional C corporations: you are, in effect, creating a new, innovative and effective business system from scratch. In this kind of system, you need to have business knowledge, industry expertise (not necessarily experience), and intuitive feel over trends in the market place. In addition, you must have a good understanding on what works in the real world and what does not (only works in theory). This is unlike in franchising or in network marketing, where systems are already in place and you are virtually guaranteed that it will work. Thus, there is less chance of failure compared to traditional Ccorporations.

Therefore, it is to be suggested that if you want to create a business system yourself, you must have at least several years of work experience in the industry that you want to grow in. Or if you do not have work experience in the industry, you must at least be engaged as a service provider by a company which is an industry player.

For example, if you want to build a Traditional C corporation, you might want to work as a broker for a few deals first or as a real estate consultant for some time. In this manner, you can be somewhat assured that your system is tried and true, with a few twists here and there. Also, you know that even though your system is brand new, it will be effective because it is a mixture or a melting pot of existing business systems in place in the industry today. If you can, look for a mentor who has been there and done that. Nonetheless, actual industry experience is not a mandatory requirement to put up a Traditional C corporation.

Chapter Five

THE FIVE LEVELS OF INVESTORS

There are five different levels or categories of investors. The people belonging in these different levels are investors from the I quadrant, although they may also earn their income simultaneously from the E quadrant, S quadrant or B quadrant.

Level 1: The Zero-Financial-Intelligence Level

The people in this level have lots and lots of money and cash flow, but for one reason or another, they fail to make reasonable returns as investors. This is because they have zero financial intelligence in the first place!

The financial intelligence of investors is a really big problem even in a country as prosperous as the USA. According to studies, more than half of the entire USA population has no financial intelligence whatsoever. Thus, any investments that they may make have negligible returns at most and, sometimes, even result to losses.

Robert Kiyosaki has a good example of a person under this

level. According to him, he has this real estate broker friend who earns a lot of cash through the commissions he enjoys by facilitating the sale between a real estate buyer and seller. He has everything one can ask for: a beautiful home in a posh village, a beautiful wife, beautiful children and expensive, luxurious cars. It is apparent that they are rich.

However, the truth is that they are poor and almost living from hand-to-mouth. All the income earned by this broker is used up to finance the luxuries they are availing. They think that these luxuries are "investments" when in fact they are not! Soon, because of this nasty habit, they become broke and, when the real estate market crashed in 2007, they become homeless.

Level 2: The Savers-Are-Losers Level

This level includes people who believe with all their heart that the key to riches and financial freedom is the old school habit of saving before spending. Investment means that you save almost all of your income by depriving yourself of all the things you want and then you devote the savings to retirement funds, bonds and other relatively stable securities.

This way, all of your expenses would be devoted to absolute essentials. Although this is a good idea in the old times when there are limited quantities of money circulating around the economy, this is no longer true now. First of all, since the currency is no longer backed by gold, the Feds can create unlimited quantities of money and circulate it to the world. Second, the act of parking your money in one place is counterproductive because inflation will eat up all its value as time goes by.

Level 3: The I'm-Too-Busy Level

This level includes university educated and professionally inclined people who are so busy and have no time whatsoever to study investments, portfolios, and risk-return ratios. Although these people have the intellectual capability to become big time investors, they cannot do so because they are so engrossed to their endeavors. This includes litigation lawyers, career politicians, surgeons and members of the police force.

Level 4: The I'm-a-Professional Level

This level usually includes people who have worked all their lives and have a big amount of cash sitting in the bank at the time of their retirement. Since they no longer have any work to do, they choose to devote all their time to studying investments and making investments. Thus, since they do investments full-time, they can be considered professional investors.

Level 5: The Capitalist Level

This level involves the richest people on the planet. Even without working, they have massive amounts of capital ready to be invested in a stock, real estate or business endeavor with a good risk-return ratio. In order to accomplish investing, the capitalist hires a team who will perform the investments for him full time. In this way, he can sit back, relax and enjoy while his investments are growing. This is the truest form of investor.

Chapter Six

YOU CANNOT SEE MONEY WITH YOUR EYES

Money Is Seen with Your Mind. What is apparent or obvious to the naked eye is not important when it comes to money matters.

For example, if you look at stocks as a form of investment, you can readily see the stock certificate, the number of shares that you hold and the price of the shares. In today's market, where stock certificates are no longer widely used, you can still see the aforesaid information on your computer screen or smart phone. However, the number of shares and its price per share is not so important when compared to the dividends that it might give, the transfer taxes that you have to pay, the capital appreciate that is possible and the return ratio that it will provide you in the coming years.

Another example is real estate. Of course, you can see the building, the windows, the doors, the office and everything that goes with it. However, these are not as important as the rental fee that it will give you (cash flow), the real estate tax that you will pay, the risk or possibility that there will be no tenant for a number of years, and the possibility that the tenant will cause damage to your property.

Thus, it is always important to look beyond what is obvious in order to determine if a given investment is worthy of your time, money and effort. Always look for what is essential and something that more than meets the eye.

In determining whether to pursue an investment or not, the following questions might help you a lot:

- Will you be willing to pay a high interest rate for such an investment?

- How long do you think you will recoup your initial investment?

- Is this investment consistent with your long term investment strategy?

- What are the factors that made you determine this investment is worthwhile?

- What is the cap rate of this investment?

- Have you included in your determination the management and employee costs?

- Did you know that the city has a new policy

21

regarding such type of businesses?

- Are you willing to pay an enormous amount of taxes in order to get this investment?

- Are you not afraid of a possible bubble or even economic recession? Will you be able to continually live in your present lifestyle should such economic disaster happen?

If all your answers to these questions are in the affirmative, then most probably you are ready to test the waters and make your investment! Just make sure that you are informed of the intricacies that surround the investment and you are good to go.

Chapter Seven

BECOMING WHO YOU ARE

The first step in changing who you presently are in order to become a financially free, content and happy person is to go through a very difficult and hard process. It is similar to a diamond undergoing a harsh process in order to become a beautiful, sharp and exquisite piece which people will covet and wear. It takes time, this is important for people to understand.

Everything is the same in becoming financially free: you must go through the process and trust in it with all your might.

The first thing to realize in order to change for the better is to treat money as a drug and to avoid getting addicted to it. When Robert Kiyosaki was a young man, rich dad always told him to not agree to get paid for work because by doing so, they will avoid money addiction. This is because people can get addicted to the regular flow of money that comes with working, what they fail to see the greater possibilities that lies ahead.

This greater possibility is none other than FINANCIAL FREEDOM.

Think about it, if you are addicted, happy and content with a minimum wage earning every year as a worker in the E quadrant, do you think your eyes will be open to earning more in the S quadrant, B quadrant and I quadrant? Of course not!

You will be so accustomed to earning money for your work that you will be blinded to anything else, including developments and improvements in your life. You will be so focused on your job, in getting by and in getting a mediocre pay that you will no longer look for what lies on the other side. In the end, this becomes an ingrained habit and it will be very difficult to break from it.

The sooner you realize this fact, the sooner you will achieve your goals.

This is why you should not get fixated in earning money for your immediate work. It is always said that one should avoid instant gratification. Well, earning immediately is one form of instant gratification because you fail to look at your future and your long term needs. This is why it is very hard to go from the E quadrant / S quadrant mindset into the B quadrant / I quadrant mindset.

Thus, instead of working for money, you should use all your intellectual capabilities and energy into devising a system of acquiring more money in the long run. You can do this by thinking that you are a player in the B quadrant / I quadrant versus a player in the E quadrant / S quadrant.

Thus, a player in the B quadrant creates and controls a unique business system where the efforts primarily come from its workforce, employees and managers. It becomes such a well-oiled system that the owner (YOU!) just has to sit back, relax and enjoy while their money is increasing by the hour.

Also, a player in the S quadrant invests cash, money and capital in a well-oiled system that is created by a player in the B quadrant. He needs not create a system himself because he just needs to find some trustworthy business partners where he can invest in. Here, he spends most of his time looking for investments which he can then fund in order for that investment to go to the next level.

Chapter Eight

HOW DO I GET RICH?

How do you get rich? If you look at it in the same way that the masses do, then by definition you probably would not get rich at all. If you want to get rich, you have to think differently than how everyone else thinks most of the time. Once you think differently, you will do differently. And once you do differently, you will have the riches that the others would not be able to have.

Now, when is the best time to think differently? The best time to think different and be different is when you are a child. Robert Kiyosaki always tells people that a child who has played and mastered the board game Monopoly has a higher chance of being financially free life compared to an adult who has no idea what the board game is.

A lot of people cannot believe that the simple act of playing the board game can give someone an edge over others. But it is not a joke. Playing Monopoly can give you tremendous advantage— the tactics and the strategies you employ in it are really doable in real life. It works in the board game and it works better in the real world!

For example, in Monopoly the objective is to buy 4 green

houses and then upgrade them into a large red hotel. Once you accumulate enough large red hotels, it is almost impossible not to get extremely wealthy. Imagine, you'll be able to command high amounts of rent in every roll of the dice of another player. This alone is very profitable even without being active in its management.

It is the same thing in the real world.

At the start, you need to buy enough assets, whether they be in the form of real estate, stocks, or business investment. Soon, it is these investments that will give you massive amounts of cash flow that, in turn, will purchase even more investments on its own. This is like a snowball that will act on its own and get bigger, better and stronger every single time.

This was the strategy used by Robert and his wife Kim in order to attain true financial freedom even if they are years and years away from the actual retirement age of 65. For instance, Robert said that he and Kim brought plenty of small family homes at the start because they had limited funds. Although it was difficult to not have money for their desires in life at that point, they persisted and invested for the future. Eventually, when their cash flow in these assets improved, they brought a large red hotel and 4 green large homes. Once this happened, they never had to work again. You can do the same!

Chapter Nine

BE THE BANK, NOT THE BANKER

The money that gets handled daily is produced by the rich—this is a general term we're using to refer to various multinational companies and large groups that have hefty stakes in the market. Now, in order to get to that point, you have to remember the formula for becoming a great player in the B quadrant and S quadrant: **BE, DO and HAVE**. Without using the *(BE – DO - HAVE)* formula together with a proper mindset towards finances, all excess money will flow out into the basket because you are just not capable of keeping it.

Thus, by **BE**-ing a person with the mindset and skill set of a great player in the B quadrant and S quadrant, you will easily recognize possible opportunities that are around you in order to DO (invest). And **DO**-ing that over and over again will result to you **HAVE**-ing the financial freedom of your dreams.

You should realize that instead of being the banker, you should become the bank. If you are the bank itself, you have the power to make massive amounts of investment into assets that will give you the desired cash flow that you need.

So how do you become a bank?

First, educate yourself. This does not mean that you need to go back to school and study business and finance. You can easily go to the local library and read books regarding finance, mortgages, real estate, and stock market valuation among others. In this way, you become more knowledgeable in the field without going through an expensive and unnecessarily stressful education. Train your mind to see through things which are not readily apparent to others.

Second, you should read books on economic history. In addition, youshould read books with respect to capitalism. In regard to this, take note of the writings and texts of the following authors, historians, businessmen and economic experts:

- Henry Ford

- JP Morgan

- John D. Rockefeller

- Robert Heilbroner

- Adam Smith

Together, these people's stories will give you a background on how a great player in the B quadrant and S quadrant should think. It also gives you an idea on how a bank (not a banker) should think. Moreover, reading their materials give you a bird eye's view over the development of Capitalism from the industrial age to its modern equivalent of specialization of efforts. This is important to determine our past and future economic trends.

So, how can you play as a bank?

Robert Kiyosaki gave a very good example of how one can play as a bank when the 1986 Tax Reform Act in the US became officially a law. The conventional feeling towards the new tax law is one of depression, pessimism and gloominess. Robert, on the other hand is optimistic that the new tax law will give him a distinct advantage over the others. This is because he thinks like a bank and not a banker.

Chapter Ten

TAKE BABY STEPS

You cannot sprint nor can you run a marathon if you cannot crawl, let alone sit. In terms of having the financial freedom of your dreams, think like a baby. Can you imagine a baby having the ability to sprint as fast as a cheetah, jump as high as a cat and swim as fast as a dolphin? No. It is the same thing when it comes to your finances, you cannot think of having a business bigger than Mark Zuckerberg's Facebook when you do not even have the skill set to manage and expand a lemonade stand on the street. Robert would even say that "A journey of a thousand miles begins with a baby step." This is consistent with the time honored principle that, "A journey of a thousand miles begins with a single step."

This needs to be emphasized because many people endeavor themselves to become trillionaires overnight without taking simple and easy steps along the way. If they cannot achieve their lofty goals in a week or in a month's effort, they become frustrated, depressed and quit on their dreams at once. This should not be the case because success takes time!

For example, many people want to lose weight quickly and

they do this by having this activity as their new year's resolution. Tens of thousands of people sign up at the gym after the 31st of December, hoping to get fit and sexy. This is the reason why fitness gyms are packed during the first week of January. By the second week of January, half of those gym goers are gone. Those who do not have the willpower to stay the course will retain their weight and level of fitness. By the month of February, everybody is gone except for those who believe in consistency, determination and perseverance in the pursuit of their goals. Again, success takes time.

Thus, instead of seeking to get really rich and have tens of millions of dollars in your bank account by tomorrow, start by taking small, easy and quick simple steps. The thing you want to avoid is to push through so hard that you crash and burn. Next thing you know you hate the process of becoming rich itself because you lacked the patience to strive a little harder.

Remember, long term financial success and financial freedom is measured not by how quick and easy you got there but by the consistency of cash flow over time together with the ability of maintaining and growing it for the duration of your career and for the remainder of your life. This is not a get rich quick scheme. This method is for the future and beyond!

THE SEVEN STEPS

TO FINDING YOUR FINANCIAL FAST TRACK

Chapter Eleven

STEP 1: IT'S TIME TO MIND YOUR OWN BUSINESS

Take Action.

For a lot of people who are struggling financially, it might become apparent that their financial statement is high on liabilities. The usual cause of this problem is that people from a very young age are socially conditioned to mind other people's business instead of minding *their own* business. This means that more and more people are following the usual dogma to work hard, save up for the future, use their credit card as much as possible to buy new stuff, then hope and pray to the high heavens that their employer will really grant them the retirement benefits which would be sufficient to cover their expenses until the day they die. All the while, this same person is making their employer, various debtors and the banks richer by the hour.

Do not be this person and start paying attention to your future!

The first thing you have to do in order to get there (financial freedom) faster is to secure a copy of a financial statement and fill it out on your own. It is important that you fill the form out on your own and not (preliminarily) seek the aid of a lawyer and an accountant to help you. This is because the form you are about to fill out is merely a prelude or preface to what is in store. Thus, it need not be exact as to the last cent so your general estimate will be sufficient for this activity.

Now, why is this important? In order to attain financial freedom, you have to first know where you are. Let us do a simple analogy.

It is like this: If you want to go to Washington DC, you have to know where you are in order to make an accurate plan on how to get to your desired destination. For example, are you in New York or California? Certainly, if you are in New York, you will get there faster (about 4-hour drive) than when you are in California (about 41-hour drive or about 10 times the distance).

Therefore, if you want financial freedom you have to know where you are right now! Whether you are a player in the E quadrant by flipping burgers in McDonald's (you are in

California) or a player in the B quadrant by owning a McDonald's franchise (you are in New York) will determine how fast you can reach your financial freedom by setting up certain and concrete short term to long term financial goals (Washington DC).

For this purpose you can make use of the guide as provided in the CASHFLOW game.

Chapter Twelve

STEP 2: TAKE CONTROL OF YOUR CASH FLOW

If you do not have the ability to control your own cash flow, then by definition you are working for somebody and you are in effect making them rich with all your efforts.

There are a lot of misconceptions about money, and one of the biggest of them all is that making more annual income, salary or profit will get the job done. However this is not true because if your costs or liabilities are on the same level, then here's a fact: you are broke!

This is because people sometimes adjust their lifestyles immediately, after being handed a lot of money. Young adults are not taught by their parents or teachers a thing or two about financial literacy. Instead, they were taught how to date, how to drive, how to ride a horse, how to swim, how to play world of Warcraft and other mundane things which aren't as useful for their financial life.

So what can you expect when that young adult ventures into his career and becomes a major player in the E quadrant / S quadrant? They can have all the positive cash flow in the world but if they cannot protect it, their financial future will be very gloomy. Without financial literacy training, they will keep on making higher and higher annual income, salary or profit to no avail.

For example, a player in the E quadrant who suddenly got promoted to Vice President of the Company and whose salary was increased ten-fold would immediately buy a house, 4 luxury cars and a trip to the Bahamas Island, to the island of Hawaii, Santorini Greece and Madrid Spain. And the worst thing is he availed most of this through the credit card! Thus, even if theoretically he became richer overnight, the money is still leaking and thus he will again be out of positive cash flow in a matter of months.

This is the reason why you have to take control your cash flow and not let it control you!

Fortunately, you are on the right track by reading this book.

Now that you have completely filled out a financial statement on your own, it is time to keep 2 sets of books.

Keeping 2 sets of books simply means this: you are somebody's asset for every liability that you have.

Look at the table below and see it for yourself:

YOUR BALANCE SHEET

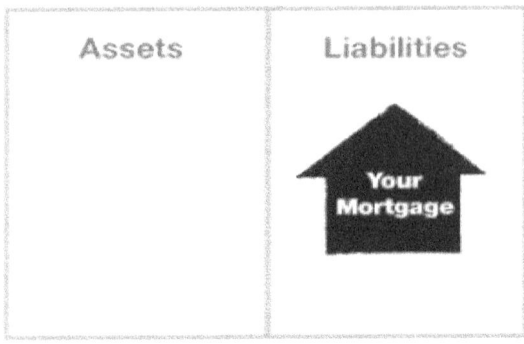

BANK'S BALANCE SHEET

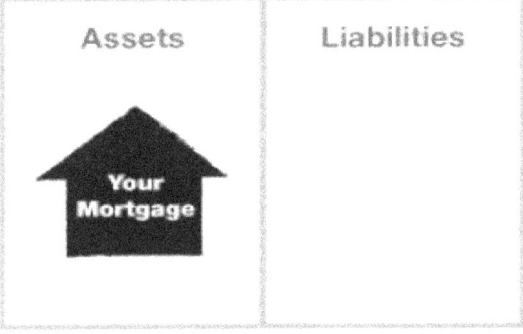

For example, let us say you have a mortgage on your house. Each month, you pay up to the mortgage lender. This payment is a liability to you (negative cash flow) and thus you are working as an asset (positive cash flow) to the mortgage lender. Your goal therefore in these 2 sets of books is to have as many assets as possible (positive cash flow).

38

Chapter Thirteen

STEP 3: KNOW THE DIFFERENCE
BETWEEN RISK AND RISKY

Knowing the difference between an asset (which gives positive cash flow) and a liability (which gives a negative cash flow) is the first key to garner the skill of proper cash flow management. The diagram below is an illustration of a properly managed cash flow of a person who is between 45 and 50 years of age:

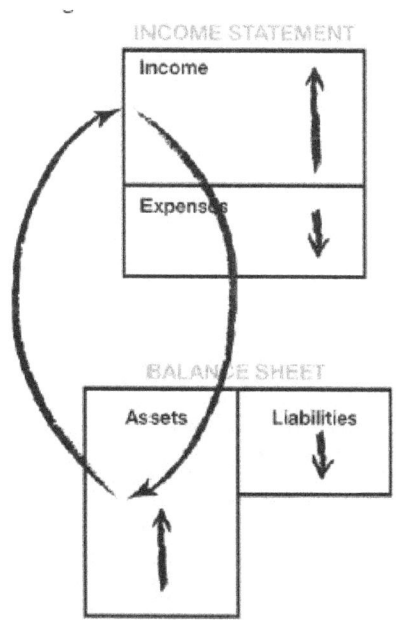

The age of between 45 and 50 years old was used because it is the midway between someone who is starting his or her career at age 22 and at the same time has at least a decade left between the normal retirement age of 65. The cash flow diagram of a person who has successfully managed his cash flow over the years by playing in the E quadrant, S quadrant, B quadrant or I quadrant simultaneously or successively should look like this. This generally means that the liabilities portion should be considerably smaller when compared to the assets portion.

This is done by avoiding unnecessary risky situation, but at the same time betting on yourself by taking calculated and educated risks towards future financial freedom.

By doing so, that person will be in the upper 10 % of the entire population and have a great chance of achieving true financial freedom in a matter of years and maintaining it throughout his/her lifetime.

On the other hand, the diagram below is one of a person who mismanages his/her cash flow by taking unnecessary risks, taking more liabilities for decades (and making the lenders rich in the process!) and accumulating little to no assets.

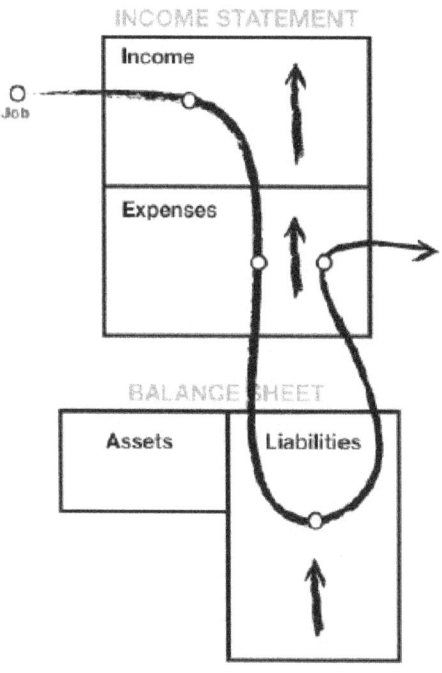

Now that you have an image of what a well-managed cash flow and mismanaged cash flow is, it is now time to determine the right amount of risk for your specific situation. You can do this by taking a piece of paper and answering the following questions:

- Do you think relying on a salary as a player in the E quadrant is risky?

- Do you think getting a loan for your house, your college or your car is risky?

- Do you think owning an asset in the form of stocks, bonds or real estate is risky?

- Do you think investing on yourself by attending trainings and seminars about financial literacy risky?

Chapter Fourteen

STEP 4: DECIDE WHAT KIND OF INVESTOR YOU WANT TO BE

It is always said that the higher the risk, the higher the reward. This saying simply means that if you bet more in your investments, then you will earn more from them. But there are people who take fewer risks, but still profit a lot. Do you know why some investors earn or profit a lot on their investments even though they are taking lower amounts of risks than others?

The reason is simple: instead of avoiding financial problems, they ACTIVELY SEEK them.

By taking financial problems, their risks are lessened because they intuitively know how to make them work. This is a form of investment in and of itself. This is different from a person who takes an investment blindly even though he knows nothing about it. The former will become financially free while the latter will suffer bankruptcy.

There are 3 basic types of investors who actively seek and take financial problems and are thus less exposed to risk:

Type A: Investors who seek problems.

These types of investors are those who seek people who are into financial trouble because of mismanagement of their financial affairs. These types of investors have a technical know-how on how to undertake a rehabilitation of the financial affairs of another. They are likewise skilled players in the S quadrant and B quadrant. Usually, they are Level-5 investors with very strong financial foundations.

The best example of these type of investors are those who participate in auction sales and foreclosure sales of properties formerly owned by another who mismanaged his/her financial affairs. Type A investors take advantage of the relatively low prices of the properties subject of auction sale or foreclosure.

Type B: Investors who seek answers.

These are types of investors who usually avail the services of insurance broker, bond agent, real estate brokers, stock brokers, investment bankers, hedge fund managers, mutual fund managers, lawyers, accountants and other consultants in order to have practical knowledge on where to spend their money on. They usually rely on the professional opinion of these people in order to come up with a decision on whether to invest in a particular product or not. The disadvantage of this is that they may be somewhat more exposed to so-called professionals who are only after their commissions.

Type C: Investors who seek an "expert" to tell them what to do.

These types of investors are usually players in the S quadrant and E quadrant who have little to no financial literacy. Thus, their investments are usually limited to retirement funds such as 401(k). They have no interest whatsoever in studying finance, tax laws and investments in order to be better investors.

Chapter Fifteen

STEP 5: SEEK MENTORS

"Mentor" refers to the person who will give you personalized and customized advice on what is essential and what is not in a given endeavor. You often meet these mentors when you are a kid and you want to join the junior school volleyball team. The coach will select students they think would be valuable to the volleyball team. Afterwards, the coach will train each individual player based on his/her strengths and weaknesses. Thus, the advice of the coach to his players is not generalized but particularized. This is to help each player grow to her highest potential. In this case, the coach is a mentor.

It is the same thing when it comes to your goal of attaining financial freedom. You need a mentor who will guide you each step of the way, will hold you by the hand to help you reach your highest possible potential, helping you instill good habits and doing away with bad habits from the get-go so you will not get frustrated when the going gets tough.

Robert Kiyosaki had a mentor and this is *rich dad*. Even though "rich dad" was not his real biological poor father, they helped Robert to reach his highest potential by training him when he was still a young boy. In this way, Robert would be able to avoid any drawbacks that could be caused by ingrained bad habits usually present in older people. This is the primary reason why Robert Kiyosaki succeeded, and this is why you should have a mentor too!

Find Someone Who's Been There

You should choose your mentors wisely. When seeking one, you should take note of what he or she has accomplished in life and whether or not this is something similar to what you want out of yours. Take note of his or her early struggles, how he/she persisted despite such challenges and how he/she handled success. Moreover, take note of how he/she maintained to keep being successful despite having the "high of success." This is because when one attains success, usually that person will rest on his laurels and stop learning and training himself. This is best exemplified by a player in the B quadrant who got rich but never worked again on his business because he already had what he wanted. As a result, his business subsequently went bankrupt. This is not what you want. Seek out a mentor who had success and maintained it for the longest time both in the B quadrant and/or S quadrant.

47

Chapter Sixteen

STEP 6: MAKE DISAPPOINTMENT YOUR STRENGTH

For every priceless gem of wisdom, there is a ton of disappointment, failures and setbacks.

When Robert Kiyosaki left the Marines for good, the first thing rich dad recommended to him, in order to jumpstart his career, was obtain the necessary skill set to get rich and to start saving up his nest egg is to work as a salesman.

Being a salesman and performing sales everyday was the last thing on Robert's mind. First, he was a shy and awkward man who did not know how to deal with people. And second, he did not like the feeling of getting rejected by people to whom he presented his product. This is because of his upbringing, during which he was inculcated to by poor dad: study hard, get good grades, then money will come to you and you do not have to do a sales job at all because it is disgusting and full of failures.

For a number of years, he was the worst sales person in the firm. He could not even close a deal with any potential client who came along. The shyness, the rejections and the setbacks were taking a toll on his psychology. Hence, he hated every minute of it and more often than not on the cusp of being fired.

This was when Robert started blaming everything – the economy, the company, the price, poor dad, rich dad, sales – everything but himself. Nevertheless, rich dad told Robert that blaming everything on another is for lame, unsuccessful and poor people. This was when Robert realized that he has victim mentality, and if he truly wanted to attain financial freedom in the B and I quadrants, he had to persist in the face of these setbacks!

From then on, Robert used the rejections he faced everyday to get him going. He used the challenges in the sales job as a fuel to get good. Instead of taking the rejections as liabilities (an opportunity to blame), he used them as an asset (a means to achieve a desired result). Eventually, he became a good salesman and learned the ropes of how to operate a business. Thus, that is the start of his journey towards financial freedom. Making mistakes is part of the game. It is completely acceptable to fail at some point and if he looks at it as an asset rather than as a liability, you will succeed! This shift in mindset alone will change your life.

Chapter Seventeen

STEP 7: THE POWER OF FAITH

There is no other person in the world who will determine your destiny other than yourself. You must keep your faith, believe in the process and trust yourself that you will make good decisions over the long haul in order to attain the ultimate objective of financial freedom. In this regard, you must continually seek to think positive thoughts and stay productive over the course of your career in the E quadrant, S quadrant, B quadrant and/or I quadrant because this will determine whether or not you will succeed.

When Robert Kiyosaki and his friend Mike (Rich dad's son) were in high school, they both had really terrible grades. Naturally, the attention of their high school teachers would go to the students who had consistent A+ grades in their class card. Robert and Mike knew early on that getting high grades is not really necessary in order to succeed in what they do. This was why simply passing was sufficient enough for them to eventually graduate in high school and move on in their lives.

The sad thing about this is that Robert and Mike's teachers

told them in high school that they will never amount to anything. They were told to get out of the class because they were the class clowns. As a result, Robert and Mike's classmates would laugh at them because of how stupid the two boys were.

Robert and Mike, instead of hating their teacher, used the event as a catalyst in order to become truly successful in their careers. Sure, the words hurt them because at the end of the day, they were kids. But early on in their lives, Robert and Mike knew that they would prove the teacher wrong and they would become successful even beyond the teacher's wildest imagination.

And this they did.

They kept faith in their beliefs and with the help of rich dad, the two attained their ultimate objective of having financial freedom. They trusted that they had what it took, and came high school reunion time, they finally proved this teacher wrong. The academic whiz kids did not amount to anything after high school. At most, they were employees of Robert and Mike's businesses, while the two clowns enjoy financial success through hard work, being smart (and not merely book smart), and trusting the process.

Chapter Eighteen

IN SUMMARY

Right now, the next step is to support yourself and your family by building pipelines of cash flow in the E quadrant, S quadrant, B quadrant and/or I quadrant.

This is the same formula that Robert and Kim used to go from zero to hero. Imagine, these two were homeless and, in the span of less than a decade, they became financially free. You can do the same if you follow the contents of this book especially the seven steps fast track outlined. Trust that the concepts and theories raised in this book are applicable in real life so you can have the things that you need and the experiences that you desire. In fact, these are the same guiding principles that Robert uses today in order to maintain his financially free status and to continually enjoy his "early retirement."

Also, be in this game for the long haul. Start becoming a long term investor. Never stop learning. Think about what you need for your life right now so you can make a plan and control your spending. Maximize your assets and limit your liabilities.

If you ingrain these habits in your life, it is only a matter of time before you can say that you are finally FINANCIALLY FREE.

Good luck.

Conclusion

The last year of active duty of Robert Kiyosaki for the Marine Corps was in 1973. At the time, he was stationed near his home in Hawaii. Upon getting back, Robert was advised by his poor dad to go back to school, finish his master's degree and work for the government until his retirement age. In other words, Poor dad wants Robert to become a player in the E quadrant and/or S quadrant.

Robert knows that poor dad wants the best for his child but he just does not know any better. Poor dad was raised in this environment and lived in this environment. Therefore, he can no longer change, certainly not at this time. As said by a famous saying, "old dogs do not learn new tricks."

Hence, although it is true that poor dad wants the best for his son, he cannot give him an advice that will benefit him. Robert knew then and there that going back to the traditional school was the farthest thing in his mind. Working for the Federal government and praying that his government retirement benefits would be sufficient until the day he died was not exciting. In fact, it was intolerable! Deep down he knew that the path to a life that he truly desires is that path carved by Rich dad and his son Mike, not the one being impressed upon him by his poor dad.

He wants to change the course, and this course he changed FOREVER.

Thus, he respectfully declined the request of his poor dad to pursue higher degrees. Instead, he pursued a kind of education like any other – an education that is not based on A's, class standing, recitations and class grades – an education that is based on true learning rather than rote memorization.

At that time, it was clear to him that traditional education is meant primarily to develop the student's mental fitness, above anything else. This is the reason why the students who are outstanding in academics usually do not do well in their personal relationships, health and finances. Robert knows that he loves education, but hates the traditional form of it. He is not made for such an environment. He realized that he could learn more outside the four corners of the classroom, than inside of it.

He signed up to attend seminars and courses regarding real estate investment, real estate valuation, investment strategies, stock market analysis, among others. He likewise attended short courses regarding marketing, sales, business development and client development. Moreover, he studied personal development, personnel management and human relations. He purchased books on Finance, Business

Management, Economics and Policy. He learned how to do business, how to make investment and how to motivate and inspire people to take action. He studied how to take advantage of business tax laws as a businessman and investor which employees and professionals do not have. He took copious notes, he researched key terms and phrases that he could not readily understand at once, and immersed himself into business and investment.

All of these are preparation to become a key player in the B quadrant and I quadrant.

This is the path to life: to become an "A" player not in school but in the B and I quadrant in order to get rich beyond your wildest imagination!

FREE BONUSES

P.S. Is it okay if we overdeliver?

Here at Readtrepreneur Publishing, we believe in overdelivering way beyond our reader's expectations. Is it okay if we overdeliver?

Here's the deal, we're going to give you an extremely condensed PDF summary of the book which you've just read and much more…

What's the catch? We need to trust you… You see, we want to overdeliver and in order for us to do that, we've to trust our reader to keep this bonus a secret to themselves? Why? Because we don't want people to be getting our exclusive PDF summaries even without buying our books itself. Unethical, right?

Ok. Are you ready?

Firstly, remember that your book is code: "**READ73**".

Next, visit this link: http://bit.ly/exclusivepdfs

Everything else will be self explanatory after you've visited: http://bit.ly/exclusivepdfs.

We hope you'll enjoy our free bonuses as much as we enjoyed preparing it for you!

CPSIA information can be obtained
at www.ICGtesting.com
Printed in the USA
LVHW092152011019
632917LV00001B/46/P

9 781646 151721